50 Italian Desserts to Make at Home

By: Kelly Johnson

Table of Contents

- Tiramisu
- Panna Cotta
- Cannoli
- Ricotta Cheesecake
- Gelato
- Biscotti
- Zabaglione
- Sfogliatelle
- Italian Almond Cookies (Amaretti)
- Semifreddo
- Italian Rainbow Cookies
- Torrone
- Struffoli
- Panettone
- Pandoro
- Zeppole
- Ricciarelli
- Budino
- Crostata di Marmellata
- Polenta Cake
- Cassata Siciliana
- Bomboloni
- Italian Cream Cake
- Torta della Nonna
- Affogato
- Italian Chocolate Salami
- Baci di Dama
- Tartufo
- Limoncello Cake
- Pistachio Gelato
- Frittelle
- Cantucci
- Sfingi
- Almond Granita
- Torta Caprese

- Italian Custard Tart
- Chocolate Ricotta Tart
- Sicilian Granita
- Stracciatella Ice Cream
- Ciambellone
- Maritozzi
- Italian Jam Cookies
- Focaccia Dolce
- Castagnaccio
- Pinza
- Mostaccioli
- Frangipane Tart
- Pastiera Napoletana
- Torta Paradiso
- Pistachio Biscotti

Tiramisu

Ingredients:

- 6 large egg yolks
- 3/4 cup granulated sugar
- 1 1/4 cups mascarpone cheese
- 1 3/4 cups heavy cream
- 2 cups strong brewed espresso, cooled
- 2 tbsp coffee liqueur (optional)
- 1 package ladyfingers
- Unsweetened cocoa powder, for dusting

Instructions:

1. Whisk egg yolks and sugar over a double boiler until thick and pale. Cool slightly, then fold in mascarpone.
2. Whip the heavy cream until stiff peaks form and fold it into the mascarpone mixture.
3. Combine espresso and liqueur. Dip each ladyfinger briefly into the mixture.
4. Layer dipped ladyfingers in a dish, followed by mascarpone cream. Repeat layers, ending with cream.
5. Dust with cocoa powder and refrigerate for at least 4 hours before serving.

Panna Cotta

Ingredients:

- 2 cups heavy cream
- 1/4 cup granulated sugar
- 1 tsp vanilla extract
- 1 packet unflavored gelatin
- 3 tbsp water
- Fresh berries or fruit compote for topping

Instructions:

1. Heat cream, sugar, and vanilla in a saucepan until sugar dissolves. Do not boil.
2. Sprinkle gelatin over water in a small bowl and let bloom for 5 minutes.
3. Stir gelatin into the warm cream mixture until completely dissolved.
4. Pour into ramekins and chill for 4-6 hours.
5. Serve with berries or compote on top.

Cannoli

Ingredients:

- **Shells:**
    - 2 cups all-purpose flour
    - 1 tbsp sugar
    - 1/4 tsp salt
    - 1 tbsp unsalted butter
    - 2 large egg yolks
    - 1/4 cup Marsala wine
    - Vegetable oil for frying
- **Filling:**
    - 2 cups ricotta cheese
    - 3/4 cup powdered sugar
    - 1/2 tsp vanilla extract
    - 1/2 cup mini chocolate chips

Instructions:

1. Combine flour, sugar, and salt. Add butter, yolks, and wine to form a dough. Chill for 30 minutes.
2. Roll dough thin, cut circles, and wrap around cannoli molds. Fry until golden.
3. Mix ricotta, powdered sugar, vanilla, and chocolate chips for filling.
4. Pipe filling into cooled shells and serve immediately.

Ricotta Cheesecake

Ingredients:

- 2 cups ricotta cheese
- 1 cup cream cheese, softened
- 3/4 cup sugar
- 3 large eggs
- 1 tsp vanilla extract
- 1/4 cup all-purpose flour
- Zest of 1 lemon

Instructions:

1. Preheat oven to 325°F (165°C). Grease a springform pan.
2. Beat ricotta, cream cheese, and sugar until smooth. Add eggs one at a time, then mix in vanilla, flour, and lemon zest.
3. Pour into the pan and bake for 50-60 minutes until set. Cool and refrigerate before serving.

Gelato

Ingredients:

- 2 cups whole milk
- 1 cup heavy cream
- 3/4 cup sugar
- 5 large egg yolks
- 1 tsp vanilla extract

Instructions:

1. Heat milk and cream in a saucepan until warm.
2. Whisk sugar and egg yolks until pale. Gradually add the warm milk to the yolks, whisking constantly.
3. Return the mixture to the saucepan and cook on low until thickened.
4. Stir in vanilla, cool, and churn in an ice cream maker.

Biscotti

Ingredients:

- 2 1/2 cups all-purpose flour
- 1 tsp baking powder
- 1/4 tsp salt
- 3/4 cup sugar
- 2 large eggs
- 1/4 cup melted butter
- 1 tsp almond extract
- 1/2 cup sliced almonds

Instructions:

1. Preheat oven to 350°F (175°C). Combine dry ingredients.
2. Beat eggs with sugar, then mix in butter and almond extract. Stir into dry ingredients with almonds.
3. Shape into logs on a baking sheet and bake for 25 minutes.
4. Slice and bake slices for 10 minutes per side until crisp.

Zabaglione

Ingredients:

- 4 large egg yolks
- 1/4 cup sugar
- 1/2 cup Marsala wine

Instructions:

1. Combine yolks and sugar in a heatproof bowl.
2. Place over simmering water and whisk until pale and thick.
3. Gradually add Marsala, whisking continuously, until the mixture doubles in volume.
4. Serve warm over fresh fruit or cake.

Sfogliatelle

Ingredients:

- **For dough:**
    - 2 cups all-purpose flour
    - 1/4 tsp salt
    - 3/4 cup water
    - 1/4 cup lard or butter
- **For filling:**
    - 1 cup ricotta
    - 1/4 cup sugar
    - 1/2 tsp cinnamon
    - 1/4 cup candied orange peel, chopped

Instructions:

1. Knead flour, salt, and water into a dough. Rest for 1 hour.
2. Roll thin, layer with lard, and fold multiple times to create layers.
3. Mix ricotta, sugar, cinnamon, and peel for filling.
4. Shape dough into cones, fill with ricotta mixture, and bake at 375°F (190°C) for 20-25 minutes.

Italian Almond Cookies (Amaretti)

Ingredients:

- 2 cups almond flour
- 1 cup powdered sugar
- 2 large egg whites
- 1/2 tsp almond extract

Instructions:

1. Preheat oven to 325°F (165°C). Line a baking sheet with parchment paper.
2. Combine almond flour and powdered sugar. Whisk egg whites until frothy and fold into the dry ingredients. Add almond extract.
3. Roll into balls and bake for 15-18 minutes until lightly golden.

Semifreddo

Ingredients:

- 4 large egg yolks
- 1/2 cup sugar
- 1 tsp vanilla extract
- 2 cups heavy cream, whipped
- Optional mix-ins: crushed cookies, fruit puree, or chocolate chips

Instructions:

1. Whisk egg yolks and sugar in a heatproof bowl over simmering water until thick and pale. Remove from heat and cool.
2. Fold in vanilla extract and whipped cream gently.
3. Add any mix-ins of your choice. Pour into a loaf pan lined with plastic wrap.
4. Freeze for at least 4-6 hours before serving.

Italian Rainbow Cookies

Ingredients:

- 1 cup almond paste
- 3/4 cup sugar
- 3/4 cup butter, softened
- 3 large eggs
- 1 cup all-purpose flour
- Food coloring (red and green)
- 1/2 cup apricot jam
- 8 oz dark chocolate, melted

Instructions:

1. Preheat oven to 350°F (175°C). Grease and line three 9x13-inch pans.
2. Cream almond paste, sugar, and butter. Add eggs and flour until smooth.
3. Divide batter into three bowls. Add red food coloring to one, green to another, and leave one plain.
4. Bake each layer for 10-12 minutes. Cool, then spread apricot jam between layers.
5. Top with melted chocolate, chill, and cut into squares.

Torrone

Ingredients:

- 2 cups sugar
- 1/2 cup honey
- 2 large egg whites
- 1/4 tsp salt
- 1 cup roasted almonds
- 1/2 cup pistachios
- Edible rice paper

Instructions:

1. Heat sugar and honey in a saucepan until dissolved and bubbling.
2. Whip egg whites with salt until stiff peaks form. Slowly pour in the hot syrup while beating continuously.
3. Fold in almonds and pistachios. Spread mixture onto a sheet of rice paper, top with another, and press gently.
4. Cool and cut into pieces.

Struffoli

Ingredients:

- 2 cups all-purpose flour
- 2 large eggs
- 2 tbsp sugar
- 1/4 tsp salt
- 2 tbsp unsalted butter, softened
- 1 tsp vanilla extract
- Honey, for coating
- Sprinkles, for decoration

Instructions:

1. Mix flour, eggs, sugar, salt, butter, and vanilla into a dough. Roll into small balls.
2. Fry the balls in hot oil until golden. Drain on paper towels.
3. Toss fried dough balls with warm honey and arrange into a mound. Sprinkle with decorations.

Panettone

Ingredients:

- 4 cups all-purpose flour
- 1/3 cup sugar
- 1/2 tsp salt
- 1 packet yeast
- 1/2 cup warm milk
- 3 large eggs
- 1/2 cup unsalted butter, softened
- 1/2 cup raisins
- 1/4 cup candied orange peel

Instructions:

1. Dissolve yeast in warm milk. Mix flour, sugar, and salt in a bowl. Add yeast, eggs, and butter to form a dough.
2. Knead in raisins and orange peel. Let rise for 2 hours.
3. Shape dough into a round loaf and place in a tall, greased mold. Let rise again.
4. Bake at 350°F (175°C) for 35-40 minutes.

Pandoro

Ingredients:

- 4 cups all-purpose flour
- 1/3 cup sugar
- 1/2 tsp salt
- 1 packet yeast
- 1/2 cup warm milk
- 3 large eggs
- 1/2 cup unsalted butter
- Powdered sugar, for dusting

Instructions:

1. Mix yeast with warm milk. Combine flour, sugar, and salt in a bowl. Add yeast mixture, eggs, and butter. Knead until smooth.
2. Let the dough rise for 2 hours. Shape into a star mold, let rise again.
3. Bake at 350°F (175°C) for 40 minutes. Cool and dust with powdered sugar.

Zeppole

Ingredients:

- 1 cup water
- 1/2 cup butter
- 1 cup all-purpose flour
- 4 large eggs
- Powdered sugar, for dusting
- Optional: pastry cream for filling

Instructions:

1. Boil water and butter in a saucepan. Stir in flour until a dough forms.
2. Remove from heat and beat in eggs one at a time.
3. Pipe dough into circles and fry in hot oil until golden.
4. Dust with powdered sugar and fill with cream if desired.

Ricciarelli

Ingredients:

- 2 cups almond flour
- 1 cup powdered sugar
- Zest of 1 orange
- 2 large egg whites
- 1/2 tsp almond extract

Instructions:

1. Preheat oven to 325°F (165°C). Line a baking sheet with parchment paper.
2. Mix almond flour, sugar, and orange zest. Whisk egg whites until stiff and fold into the mixture. Add almond extract.
3. Shape into oval cookies and bake for 15-20 minutes.

Budino

Ingredients:

- 2 cups whole milk
- 1/2 cup sugar
- 1/4 cup cornstarch
- 1/4 cup unsweetened cocoa powder (optional)
- 1 tsp vanilla extract

Instructions:

1. Heat milk in a saucepan. Mix sugar, cornstarch, and cocoa powder (if using). Gradually whisk into the milk.
2. Cook on medium heat until thickened. Remove from heat and stir in vanilla.
3. Pour into ramekins, cool, and refrigerate for 2 hours before serving.

Crostata di Marmellata (Jam Tart)

Ingredients:

- 2 1/2 cups all-purpose flour
- 1/2 cup sugar
- 1/2 tsp salt
- 1/2 cup unsalted butter, chilled
- 2 large eggs
- 1 tsp vanilla extract
- 1 cup fruit jam (e.g., apricot, raspberry)

Instructions:

1. Combine flour, sugar, and salt. Cut in butter until crumbly. Add eggs and vanilla, forming a dough. Chill for 30 minutes.
2. Roll out dough and press into a tart pan. Spread jam evenly over the base.
3. Use remaining dough to create lattice strips on top.
4. Bake at 350°F (175°C) for 25-30 minutes or until golden.

Polenta Cake

Ingredients:

- 1 1/4 cups almond flour
- 1/2 cup polenta (cornmeal)
- 1 tsp baking powder
- 3/4 cup sugar
- 1/2 cup unsalted butter, softened
- 3 large eggs
- Zest of 1 lemon

Instructions:

1. Preheat oven to 350°F (175°C). Grease a round cake pan.
2. Cream butter and sugar until fluffy. Add eggs one at a time. Mix in almond flour, polenta, baking powder, and lemon zest.
3. Pour batter into the pan and bake for 35-40 minutes. Cool before serving.

Cassata Siciliana

Ingredients:

- 1 sponge cake (8-inch round)
- 2 cups ricotta cheese
- 1 cup powdered sugar
- 1/2 cup candied fruit, diced
- 1/4 cup mini chocolate chips
- Marzipan and icing for decoration

Instructions:

1. Beat ricotta with sugar until smooth. Fold in candied fruit and chocolate chips.
2. Slice sponge cake into layers and line a round mold with one layer. Fill with ricotta mixture and top with another layer.
3. Chill for 2 hours. Decorate with marzipan and icing before serving.

Bomboloni (Italian Donuts)

Ingredients:

- 2 1/2 cups all-purpose flour
- 1/4 cup sugar
- 1/2 tsp salt
- 1 packet yeast
- 3/4 cup warm milk
- 2 large eggs
- 1/4 cup unsalted butter, melted
- Oil for frying
- Sugar for coating

Instructions:

1. Mix flour, sugar, salt, and yeast. Add warm milk, eggs, and melted butter to form a dough. Let rise for 1 hour.
2. Roll dough and cut into circles. Let rise again for 30 minutes.
3. Fry in hot oil until golden. Drain and coat in sugar. Fill with cream or jam if desired.

Italian Cream Cake

Ingredients:

- 2 cups all-purpose flour
- 1 tsp baking powder
- 1/2 tsp baking soda
- 1 cup sugar
- 1/2 cup unsalted butter, softened
- 3 large eggs
- 1 cup buttermilk
- 1/2 cup shredded coconut
- 1/2 cup chopped pecans
- Cream cheese frosting

Instructions:

1. Preheat oven to 350°F (175°C). Grease and flour two round cake pans.
2. Cream butter and sugar. Add eggs one at a time. Mix in dry ingredients alternately with buttermilk. Fold in coconut and pecans.
3. Bake for 25-30 minutes. Cool and frost with cream cheese frosting.

Torta della Nonna (Grandmother's Cake)

Ingredients:

- 2 cups all-purpose flour
- 1/2 cup sugar
- 1/2 tsp salt
- 1/2 cup unsalted butter, chilled
- 2 large eggs
- 1 cup pastry cream
- Pine nuts and powdered sugar for topping

Instructions:

1. Prepare pastry dough with flour, sugar, salt, butter, and eggs. Chill for 30 minutes.
2. Roll out and line a tart pan. Fill with pastry cream.
3. Top with pine nuts and bake at 350°F (175°C) for 25-30 minutes. Cool and dust with powdered sugar.

Affogato

Ingredients:

- 2 scoops vanilla gelato or ice cream
- 1 shot hot espresso

Instructions:

1. Place gelato in a serving glass.
2. Pour hot espresso over the gelato. Serve immediately.

Italian Chocolate Salami

Ingredients:

- 8 oz dark chocolate, melted
- 1/2 cup crushed biscuits or cookies
- 1/4 cup almonds, chopped
- 1/4 cup pistachios, chopped
- 2 tbsp cocoa powder
- Powdered sugar for coating

Instructions:

1. Mix melted chocolate with crushed biscuits, almonds, pistachios, and cocoa powder.
2. Shape into a log, wrap in plastic, and chill for 2 hours.
3. Roll in powdered sugar before slicing.

Baci di Dama (Lady's Kisses)

Ingredients:

- 1 cup almond flour
- 3/4 cup all-purpose flour
- 1/2 cup sugar
- 1/2 cup unsalted butter, softened
- 3 oz dark chocolate, melted

Instructions:

1. Mix almond flour, all-purpose flour, sugar, and butter into a dough. Chill for 30 minutes.
2. Roll into small balls and bake at 350°F (175°C) for 10-12 minutes. Cool.
3. Sandwich two cookies with melted chocolate in between.

Tartufo (Italian Ice Cream Dessert)

Ingredients:

- 2 cups chocolate ice cream
- 2 cups vanilla ice cream
- 1/4 cup cocoa powder
- 1/4 cup chocolate shavings
- 1/2 cup maraschino cherries (optional)

Instructions:

1. Scoop vanilla ice cream and place a cherry in the center. Cover with chocolate ice cream to form a ball.
2. Freeze for 1 hour. Roll in cocoa powder and chocolate shavings. Freeze until firm.
3. Serve chilled.

Limoncello Cake

Ingredients:

- 1 1/2 cups all-purpose flour
- 1 tsp baking powder
- 1/4 tsp salt
- 3/4 cup sugar
- 1/2 cup unsalted butter, softened
- 2 large eggs
- 1/4 cup limoncello
- Zest of 1 lemon

Instructions:

1. Preheat oven to 350°F (175°C). Grease a round cake pan.
2. Cream butter and sugar. Add eggs, one at a time. Mix in limoncello and lemon zest.
3. Fold in flour, baking powder, and salt. Bake for 30-35 minutes. Cool and dust with powdered sugar.

Pistachio Gelato

Ingredients:

- 1 1/2 cups whole milk
- 1/2 cup heavy cream
- 1/2 cup sugar
- 1/2 cup pistachio paste
- 4 egg yolks

Instructions:

1. Heat milk and cream until warm. Whisk egg yolks and sugar until creamy. Gradually mix in warm milk.
2. Cook over low heat until thickened. Stir in pistachio paste.
3. Chill mixture, then churn in an ice cream maker. Freeze until firm.

Frittelle (Italian Fritters)

Ingredients:

- 1 cup all-purpose flour
- 1/4 cup sugar
- 1/2 tsp baking powder
- 1/4 tsp salt
- 1/2 cup milk
- 1 large egg
- Oil for frying
- Powdered sugar for dusting

Instructions:

1. Mix flour, sugar, baking powder, and salt. Add milk and egg to form a batter.
2. Heat oil and drop spoonfuls of batter into the oil. Fry until golden.
3. Drain and dust with powdered sugar.

Cantucci (Italian Biscotti)

Ingredients:

- 2 cups all-purpose flour
- 1 tsp baking powder
- 3/4 cup sugar
- 1/2 tsp salt
- 1/2 cup almonds, whole
- 2 large eggs
- Zest of 1 orange

Instructions:

1. Preheat oven to 350°F (175°C). Mix flour, sugar, baking powder, and salt. Add eggs and orange zest. Stir in almonds.
2. Shape dough into a log and bake for 20 minutes. Cool slightly, slice, and bake again until crisp.

Sfingi (Italian Ricotta Donuts)

Ingredients:

- 1 cup ricotta cheese
- 2 large eggs
- 1/4 cup sugar
- 1 cup all-purpose flour
- 1 tsp baking powder
- 1/4 tsp salt
- Oil for frying
- Powdered sugar for coating

Instructions:

1. Mix ricotta, eggs, and sugar until smooth. Add flour, baking powder, and salt.
2. Drop spoonfuls of batter into hot oil. Fry until golden and drain.
3. Coat with powdered sugar before serving.

Almond Granita

Ingredients:

- 2 cups almond milk
- 1/4 cup sugar
- 1/2 tsp almond extract

Instructions:

1. Combine almond milk, sugar, and almond extract. Stir until sugar dissolves.
2. Pour into a shallow dish and freeze. Scrape with a fork every hour to create granita texture. Serve cold.

Torta Caprese (Chocolate Almond Cake)

Ingredients:

- 1 cup almond flour
- 1 cup dark chocolate, melted
- 1/2 cup sugar
- 1/2 cup unsalted butter, softened
- 4 large eggs
- 1/4 cup cocoa powder

Instructions:

1. Preheat oven to 350°F (175°C). Grease a round cake pan.
2. Cream butter and sugar. Add eggs one at a time. Mix in melted chocolate, almond flour, and cocoa powder.
3. Pour into the pan and bake for 25-30 minutes. Cool before serving.

Italian Custard Tart (Torta alla Crema)

Ingredients:

- 2 cups all-purpose flour
- 1/2 cup sugar
- 1/2 tsp salt
- 1/2 cup unsalted butter, chilled
- 2 large eggs
- 2 cups pastry cream

Instructions:

1. Prepare pastry dough with flour, sugar, salt, butter, and eggs. Chill for 30 minutes.
2. Roll out dough and press into a tart pan. Fill with pastry cream.
3. Bake at 350°F (175°C) for 25-30 minutes. Cool before serving.

Chocolate Ricotta Tart

Ingredients:

- 1 pie crust (store-bought or homemade)
- 1 1/2 cups ricotta cheese
- 1/2 cup sugar
- 1/4 cup cocoa powder
- 2 large eggs
- 1/2 tsp vanilla extract
- 1/4 cup dark chocolate chips

Instructions:

1. Preheat oven to 350°F (175°C). Line a tart pan with the pie crust.
2. Beat ricotta, sugar, cocoa powder, eggs, and vanilla until smooth. Fold in chocolate chips.
3. Pour filling into the crust and bake for 30–35 minutes. Cool before serving.

Sicilian Granita

Ingredients:

- 2 cups water
- 1/2 cup sugar
- 1 cup fresh fruit juice (e.g., lemon, orange, or strawberry)

Instructions:

1. Heat water and sugar until dissolved. Cool and mix in fruit juice.
2. Pour into a shallow dish and freeze. Scrape with a fork every 30 minutes to create a granita texture. Serve icy.

Stracciatella Ice Cream

Ingredients:

- 2 cups whole milk
- 1 cup heavy cream
- 3/4 cup sugar
- 4 large egg yolks
- 1/4 cup dark chocolate, melted

Instructions:

1. Heat milk, cream, and sugar until warm. Whisk egg yolks and slowly add warm milk mixture.
2. Cook on low heat until thickened. Cool and churn in an ice cream maker. Drizzle in melted chocolate while churning to create stracciatella shards.

Ciambellone (Italian Ring Cake)

Ingredients:

- 2 cups all-purpose flour
- 1 tsp baking powder
- 1/4 tsp salt
- 3/4 cup sugar
- 1/2 cup olive oil
- 3 large eggs
- 1/2 cup milk
- Zest of 1 lemon

Instructions:

1. Preheat oven to 350°F (175°C). Grease a bundt or ring cake pan.
2. Mix flour, baking powder, and salt. In a separate bowl, beat sugar, olive oil, eggs, milk, and lemon zest.
3. Combine wet and dry ingredients. Pour into the pan and bake for 35–40 minutes. Cool before serving.

Maritozzi (Italian Sweet Cream Buns)

Ingredients:

- 3 cups all-purpose flour
- 1/4 cup sugar
- 1 tsp salt
- 1 packet active dry yeast
- 3/4 cup warm milk
- 1/4 cup unsalted butter, melted
- 2 large eggs
- 1 cup whipped cream (for filling)

Instructions:

1. Mix flour, sugar, salt, and yeast. Add warm milk, melted butter, and eggs to form a dough. Knead until smooth. Let rise for 1 hour.
2. Shape into small buns and place on a baking sheet. Let rise for 30 minutes.
3. Bake at 350°F (175°C) for 15–20 minutes. Cool, then slice and fill with whipped cream.

Italian Jam Cookies (Occhi di Bue)

Ingredients:

- 2 cups all-purpose flour
- 1/2 cup sugar
- 1/2 tsp salt
- 1/2 cup unsalted butter, chilled
- 1 large egg
- 1/2 cup fruit jam (e.g., apricot or raspberry)

Instructions:

1. Preheat oven to 350°F (175°C). Mix flour, sugar, and salt. Cut in butter, then add the egg to form a dough. Chill for 30 minutes.
2. Roll out and cut into circles. Cut smaller circles out of half the cookies for the tops.
3. Bake for 10–12 minutes. Cool and assemble with jam between layers.

Focaccia Dolce (Sweet Focaccia)

Ingredients:

- 3 cups all-purpose flour
- 1 tsp salt
- 1/4 cup sugar
- 1 packet active dry yeast
- 3/4 cup warm water
- 1/4 cup olive oil
- 1/4 cup raisins
- 2 tbsp honey (for drizzling)

Instructions:

1. Mix flour, salt, sugar, and yeast. Add water and olive oil to form a dough. Knead until smooth and let rise for 1 hour.
2. Flatten dough onto a baking sheet. Sprinkle raisins on top. Let rise for another 30 minutes.
3. Bake at 375°F (190°C) for 20–25 minutes. Drizzle with honey before serving.

Castagnaccio (Chestnut Flour Cake)

Ingredients:

- 2 cups chestnut flour
- 1 1/2 cups water
- 1/4 cup olive oil
- 1/4 cup raisins
- 2 tbsp pine nuts
- 1 tbsp rosemary leaves
- Pinch of salt

Instructions:

1. Preheat oven to 375°F (190°C). Grease a round cake pan.
2. Sift chestnut flour into a bowl and gradually whisk in water to form a smooth batter.
3. Stir in olive oil, raisins, and a pinch of salt. Pour into the prepared pan.
4. Sprinkle pine nuts and rosemary on top. Bake for 25–30 minutes.

Pinza (Venetian Holiday Cake)

Ingredients:

- 2 cups all-purpose flour
- 1 cup cornmeal
- 1/2 cup sugar
- 1/4 cup raisins
- 1/4 cup dried figs, chopped
- 1/4 cup almonds, chopped
- 2 tsp anise seeds
- 1 tsp baking powder
- 1/2 cup milk
- 1/2 cup butter, melted
- Zest of 1 lemon

Instructions:

1. Preheat oven to 350°F (175°C). Grease a loaf pan.
2. Combine dry ingredients in a bowl. Mix milk, melted butter, and lemon zest in a separate bowl.
3. Fold wet ingredients into dry ingredients and stir in raisins, figs, almonds, and anise seeds.
4. Pour into the pan and bake for 40–45 minutes.

Mostaccioli (Spiced Cookies)

Ingredients:

- 2 cups all-purpose flour
- 1/2 cup sugar
- 1/2 tsp ground cinnamon
- 1/4 tsp ground cloves
- 1/4 tsp ground nutmeg
- 1/4 cup honey
- 1/4 cup water
- 1/4 cup dark chocolate, melted

Instructions:

1. Preheat oven to 350°F (175°C). Mix flour, sugar, and spices in a bowl.
2. Heat honey and water until combined, then mix into the dry ingredients to form a dough.
3. Roll out dough and cut into diamond shapes. Place on a baking sheet and bake for 12–15 minutes.
4. Cool and drizzle with melted chocolate.

Frangipane Tart

Ingredients:

- 1 pie crust
- 1/2 cup almond flour
- 1/4 cup butter, softened
- 1/4 cup sugar
- 1 large egg
- 1/2 tsp almond extract
- Fresh fruit or jam for topping

Instructions:

1. Preheat oven to 350°F (175°C). Line a tart pan with the pie crust.
2. Beat almond flour, butter, sugar, egg, and almond extract until creamy. Spread over the crust.
3. Arrange fruit or jam on top. Bake for 25–30 minutes until golden.

Pastiera Napoletana (Neapolitan Easter Pie)

Ingredients:

- 1 pie crust
- 2 cups ricotta cheese
- 1/2 cup sugar
- 1/4 cup cooked wheat grains or rice
- 2 large eggs
- Zest of 1 orange
- 1/2 tsp cinnamon

Instructions:

1. Preheat oven to 350°F (175°C). Line a tart pan with the pie crust.
2. Mix ricotta, sugar, wheat grains, eggs, orange zest, and cinnamon until smooth. Pour into the crust.
3. Bake for 45–50 minutes. Cool before serving.

Torta Paradiso (Paradise Cake)

Ingredients:

- 1 cup all-purpose flour
- 1/2 cup cornstarch
- 1 cup sugar
- 1/2 cup butter, softened
- 3 large eggs
- 1 tsp vanilla extract
- 1 tsp baking powder
- Powdered sugar for dusting

Instructions:

1. Preheat oven to 350°F (175°C). Grease a cake pan.
2. Beat butter and sugar until fluffy. Add eggs one at a time, then mix in vanilla.
3. Combine flour, cornstarch, and baking powder, and fold into the wet mixture.
4. Pour batter into the pan and bake for 30–35 minutes. Dust with powdered sugar.

Pistachio Biscotti

Ingredients:

- 2 cups all-purpose flour
- 1 tsp baking powder
- 1/4 tsp salt
- 1/2 cup sugar
- 2 large eggs
- 1/2 tsp vanilla extract
- 1/2 cup pistachios

Instructions:

1. Preheat oven to 350°F (175°C). Mix flour, baking powder, salt, and sugar.
2. Beat eggs and vanilla, then mix into dry ingredients to form a dough. Fold in pistachios.
3. Shape dough into a log and bake for 20 minutes. Cool slightly, then slice into biscotti.
4. Bake slices for another 10–12 minutes until crisp.